THE HEREFORD
MAPPA MUNDI

THE HEREFORD
MAPPA MUNDI

Gabriel Alington

Illustrations by
Dominic Harbour

Gracewing.

First published in 1996
Reprinted 2000

Gracewing
2 Southern Avenue, Leominster
Herefordshire, HR6 0QF

ISBN 0 85244 355 2

Designed and typeset by RM Graphic Design, Llangunllo, Powys.
Printed by Cromwell Press, Trowbridge, Wiltshire.

Contents

Here be
DRAGONS!

The medieval world-view

A MAP OF THE WORLD, a geographic diagram of land and sea; that is how we think of it nowadays. But in the Middle Ages a Mappa Mundi, a map of the world - as much of it as was known then - contained far more than a modern map. It was packed with information; history, legend, the wonders of nature, stories from the Bible; everything was there, set out within the map in words and pictures, an encyclopaedic study of the world. An 'estoire' was a description sometimes used, which translates as a story, the story of the world. Medieval world maps followed a tradition of map making established in Roman times. When, in the fifth century, barbarians swept through Western Europe there was huge destruction; many works of learning were destroyed. But monks and scholars struggled bravely to salvage what they could and, through the dark years that followed, succeeding generations kept them safe.

In the Middle Ages map makers made use of this ancient learning. They gathered it together and studied it; they sifted, compiled and redefined. Most importantly they adapted it all to a Christian point of view. A medieval encyclopaedic map represented the world in biblical

Below / The Tripartite form of world maps put east at the top and bisected the globe with a T-shape which divided the three continental masses of Africa, Europe and Asia.

Asia

Europe   Africa

terms. There were many variations; round maps, square maps, maps with the east positioned at the top, others with the north up there instead. Some included a fourth continent, the Antipodes, others, the majority, left it out. Indeed, according to some scholars, a world of four continents was a heresy, out of line with the Christian view. The form that fitted the Christian interpretation most conveniently was known as the Tripartite map. The world, enclosed within a circle, was divided by a T-shape which separated the three continents. Asia was at the top, above the bar of the T, Europe to the left and Africa to the right. The T-shape was said to represent the crucifixion, the three continents the descent of man from the three sons of Noah[1]. East was generally at the top and, in later maps, Jerusalem[2] was right in the middle, the City of God in the centre of the world.

Most of the early world maps[3] were on a small scale and were probably used to illustrate books. Encyclopaedic studies by scholars such as Orosius, who lived in the fifth century and was a student of St. Augustine, were popular in the Middle Ages. And perhaps an accompanying map would have helped to bring the words to life. Certainly the catalogues of medieval libraries include many references to world maps. Over a thousand have survived, some from as early as the seventh century. Very few are complete; most are fragments, fragile and torn, their colours faded with age and exposure to light. A rare exception is the diminutive Psalter Map which measures less than ten centimetres across. It was made in about 1260 and is probably a copy of a much larger map produced for Henry III. Perhaps because of its royal connection it was treated with particular care for it has kept its colour remarkably. The maps were painted with colours made from vegetable dyes, sometimes with touches of gold and silver leaf. The jewel brightness of the illuminated capital letters in carefully preserved medieval books gives a clue to how the maps appeared originally. At the beginning of the twelfth century mappa mundi on a much larger scale began to be produced. These were intended as wall maps and were made of cloth; the literal meaning of 'mappa mundi' is 'cloth of the world'. In some cases a map was painted directly onto a wall.

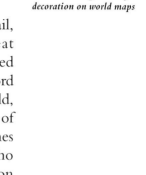

Above / Medieval illuminated manuscripts give some idea of the colour and brightness of the decoration on world maps

The size of a wall map allowed for more detail, more information and illustrations. A great assortment of creatures and mythical beasts pranced through the world of these larger maps; the Hereford Mappa has a feast of them. The lay-out of that world, its geography, varied widely. The same was true of the earlier smaller maps and may have sometimes been due to the scribes who worked on them, who perhaps could not read and so copied parrot fashion without understanding what they wrote and drew. Occasionally whole continents were switched about. But with so little of the world properly charted and vast areas completely unknown, geography was anyhow partly a matter of guesswork. Few people, even men of learning, can have questioned the way countries and oceans were squeezed and stretched to fit within a circle.

What was important, and markedly more so in theses later maps, was to set out the world in Christian terms. The aim was to show the whole of God's creation, past and present, in a geographic frame. The total concept, we might call it now. And, as if to emphasise this, in almost every case, God would be pictured above the world, in Paradise. Alternately, as in the enormous Ebstorf Map, sadly destroyed in the Second World War, God would completely surround the world, leaving no doubt it belonged to him. Generally there was a separate text which

Above / Scribes with little learning themselves were apt to make confusing mistakes in copying the texts and illustrations.

FOCUS

Chaucer wrote as he spoke in Middle English:

'O blisful light, of which the bemes clere adorneth al the thridde heven faire!'

– TROILUS AND CRISEIDE

Below / Paris, whose university was one of the earliest in Europe

referred to the learning in the map and was often written by its designer. As a rule he was a professional map maker, a cartographer, who would have employed scribes and illuminators to carry out the work. Occasionally Norman French crops up in the texts of the larger maps but, predominantly, as in all scholarly medieval writing, Latin was used. Increasingly poetry and prose was written in Middle English, the language of everyday speech. Geoffrey Chaucer, for example, wrote as he spoke. But the type of courtly romance read by the aristocracy was written in Norman French for that was their tongue.

And, for the most part, it was the aristocracy who owned wall maps. They were prestige objects. A mappa mundi in your private chapel or the audience chamber of your palace or castle proved you to be a man of stature, a man of learning and considerable wealth - wall maps did not come cheap. Often the designer would be asked to decorate the surrounding border to suit the owner, perhaps with pictures representing his life and achievements. In some cases this was used as a form of self promotion. Prominently displayed behind the throne of the king, or the high seat of some powerful baron, a great mappa mundi proclaiming his conquests provided an impressive backdrop. Here was a man to be reckoned with.

But not all wall maps were privately owned. They were hung in public places, in churches, in colleges of education. For that was their main purpose, to teach, to encourage learning. And in the twelfth and thirteenth centuries the opportunities for learning were increasing. All over Europe universities were being established, Bologna, Paris, Oxford, Cambridge. And those were only the first of them.

It was a time of expansion, a time when the living conditions of working people gradually improved.

Under feudal law, which existed throughout most of Europe, each person owed allegiance to their overlord. There were still many who were born 'unfree' and who remained so all their lives. Nonetheless, in England, the rights established by Magna Carta did eventually filter down to the poorest labourers, the great

Below / Harvest time in the 13th century

majority who made their living on the land. With better conditions the population grew at a steady pace. Between 1186 and 1300 it doubled to three million.

More land was needed for cultivation so woodland was dug up, heath and moorland cleared, in the Fen country marshes were drained. And, as methods of farming became less primitive, production rose. This improvement was, to a large extent, due to a book on farm management published in 1259. The ideas put forward by Walter of Henly in his *Book of Husbandry* were widely followed and found to be effective.

As time went by people moved into the towns, a trickle at first, then a growing tide. Towns and cities spread rapidly: Bristol, Plymouth, Coventry, York, and London most of all. In some ways urban living conditions were worse than those of the countryside. Town life was crowded, dirty, noisy; criminals thrived, so did the rats, spreading disease as fast as the fires that could rage unchecked through the narrow streets. On the other hand town-dwellers were free of feudalism. They owed allegiance, that is loyalty and obedience, to the Mayor and his councillors rather than to the Lord of the Manor. Besides town life moved at a faster pace, there was bustle and excitement. There was also entertainment, a wide variety: street theatre, mummers,

FOCUS

Walter of Henly's Book of Husbandry *introduced improved farming practice which markedly increased production.*

Below / Performing bear

FOCUS

Most importantly, in towns there was employment. As well as jobs that supported everyday existence: baking, tailoring, guarding the walls and gates of the towns, there were industries, weaving, coopering and leather working.

musicians, dancing bears, and generally of a far higher standard than the self-made efforts of the countryside. Most importantly, in towns there was employment. As well as jobs that supported everyday existence, baking, tailoring, guarding the walls and gates of the town, there were industries, weaving, coopering and leather working. Towns tended to specialise in an industry suited to the locality. Fulling, for example, the washing and extraction of grease from wool fleece, was mainly carried out in Yorkshire and the Lake District where there was a plentiful supply of water. Then the fleeces were transported in horse-drawn wagons to surrounding towns for spinning, weaving and finally dyeing. Guilds were set up by the craftsmen of each trade to monitor the quality of the goods produced and oversee the training of apprentices. The Guilds also protected the workers' rights in a similar way to the present day trade unions. And, like them, the medieval Guilds wielded considerable influence. Goods were marketed at trade fairs that took place all over the country and usually lasted for about three weeks. They were eagerly awaited, an excuse for an outing and, once the serious business of trading was done, for a good deal of merry making and imbibing of profits. It was the wool fairs that attracted the greatest crowds, and, as the wool trade prospered they grew in size and popularity. Around the flat sheep farming country of Huntingdon and Lincolnshire they became major events, combining commerce with festivity. Fairs were rich hunting grounds for thieves who, mingling with the crowds, could do as well as any trader. In the Champagne district of France, where the fairs were famously merry, the ruling counts employed market bailiffs to protect the merchants from thieving and corruption.

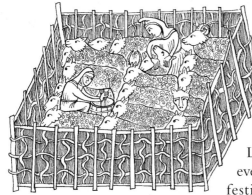

Above / Farm workers preparing sheep for a country wool fair.

Left / Edward I

Throughout the Middle Ages international trade grew steadily. England, with wool as its prime export, had to face competition from Spain. But the quality of the English cloth, as well as the fleeces that were shipped across to Flanders to be woven, ensured a high demand. The scarlet cloth of Lincoln was said to be the finest in the world.

At the end of the 13th century Edward I, who had earlier borrowed money from the bankers of Italy, Europe's leading financiers, to pay for his expanding government, recruited their help in handling the export of English wool.

But wool was not the only commodity. From the countries of Europe there was wine, grain, olive oil, salt; furs were shipped across the Baltic Sea, and from far to the south came silks, spices, ivory, gold. Venice was a central trading port, 'the gateway to the East', a junction where merchants from Europe met to do business with those from Asia and Africa.

Left and Below / An Astrolabe and other early navigation instruments

Later mappa mundi mark these trade routes, the itineraries of merchants. Such journeys could last for many months. Travel by sea was hazardous. Navigation was determined by astrolabe, an instrument invented by the Arabs which measured the position of the sun, or simply by the stars. But small wooden vessels, powered by sail, were all too easily blown off course and battered by storms. And there were pirates about, roaming the seas on the lookout for laden merchantmen.

On land the dangers were no less great. Robbers

lay in wait along every route and travellers would often hire armed guards to accompany them. Roads were dirt tracks, rutted and potholed, and, in bad weather, deep in mud. Even when conditions were good it would be rare to cover more than thirty kilometres in one day. With a horse-drawn wagon piled with goods progress was slower still. Merchants trekking overland from Bruges to Venice would have to allow at least four weeks.

Yet, despite the hazards, travel was very much part of life. There was constant movement from place to place, on horseback, on foot. News was carried by messenger. Friars, often barefoot, crook in hand, would trudge round villages preaching and collecting alms. Often, when the drains became overloaded, nobles moved their entire household from one castle to another. Crusaders journeyed to the Holy Land. Their itineraries, as well as those of pilgrims, are shown on some of the later world maps. Pilgrimages were made to a number of shrines; to Jerusalem, to St Peter's in Rome, to St James' in Compostella in Spain, to St Thomas a Becket's in Canterbury. Many people from very varied backgrounds went on pilgrimages. Some travelled alone, others went in parties. Chaucer's Canterbury Tales brings one group of them vividly to life. And, though the principal reason for going was to pray at the holy shrine, a pilgrimage could also be a holiday. It was a break from work, a chance to travel in company, to stop off at inns to eat and sleep. No wonder they were popular. And, like present day tourists, as soon as they arrived pilgrims would be besieged by local traders selling souvenirs; holy pictures, relics such as locks of hair, fragments of bone, from the sacred body of the saint of course, guaranteed to bring eternal benefit. The greatest mass movement of people happened when an army was on the march, an impressive sight with the

Below / Rome sits in magnificence astride the Tiber

knights on horseback in their bright coloured surcoats, their banners held high. This was a frequent occurrence during the turbulent years that followed the signing of Magna Carta when the barons rebelled against the King, and again during the reign of Edward I who fought a series of campaigns in both Scotland and Wales. In Scotland he eventually defeated the rebel leader William Wallace at Falkirk in 1298, while in Wales he won control of the whole principality. Two of the great castles he built to mark his conquests, Conway and Caernavon, are pictured on the Hereford Mappa Mundi.

Left / A rather sparsely populated Wales

Campaigns were also fought abroad, mainly in France, which meant that large numbers of troops were shipped across the Channel. It was the ongoing friction between England and France over the sovereignty of Normandy and Gascony that led to the Hundred Years' War.

And always, in the air, a kind of restlessness, an urge to push beyond the known world, to search out new trade routes, discover regions as yet unnamed. In many cases explorers were sponsored by a king, for, among the rival European powers, there was keen competition to claim these virgin territories for their own. The most successful expeditions were made in the late Middle Ages, towards the end of the 15th Century, when two Italians, Christopher Columbus and John Cabot, discovered lands across the Atlantic. In 1492 Columbus, who was sponsored by King Ferdinand of Spain, reached the West Indies; in 1497 Cabot, as he is generally known, landed on Cape Breton Island off the coast of Canada. Heading southwards, in 1488 the Portuguese adventurer, Bartholomew Diaz, sailed round the Cape of Good Hope. Twenty

FOCUS

The most successful expeditions of exploration were made in the late Middle Ages, towards the end of the 15th Century...

years later his fellow countryman, Vasco da Gama, sponsored by his king, Manuel I, led his ships further still, right to the southern tip of India.

There were many others. And many who did not come back. Perhaps they struck bad weather and were lost at sea. Perhaps, it was thought by many people then, they had sailed too far, beyond the limits of the great flat world and fallen off the edge. For, though there were some who suspected it, no one then was sure that the world was round. Not until the 16th century, when, in 1520, the Portuguese explorer, Ferdinand Magellan, on his final voyage, sailed through the straits that were named for him, did the truth become clear.

✤

B A C K G R O U N D

Journey to
HEREFORD

The history of the Mappa Mundi

Above / A Griffin, bearing a marked similarity to a winged Welsh dragon

T HE HEREFORD MAPPA MUNDI IS UNIQUE. It is the only complete wall map of the world known to have survived from the Middle Ages. Perhaps one reason for its durability is that it was drawn on vellum, a type of leather which is fine but strong. And a single skin was used, no seams, no joins. It measures 64 inches from top to bottom and 54 inches across.

The black ink, which was probably mineral based, is still sharp and strong. But the brightness of the paint, the different vegetable dyes, has for the most part dulled and merged so that the overall impression is of ochre brown, the sepia of very old photographs. In places the red is still distinct; there is even the faintest glint of gold, but small, so small you think perhaps you have imagined it.

For there is something mysterious about the Map. It has a presence of its own, shadowy almost mystical, set apart by time. But it cannot be ignored, nor glanced at briefly as you wander past. It demands your attention; it is there to teach, to give out its wisdom, to draw you into its ancient world. Yet there is so much about it that re-mains unknown. When was it made?

No one can be sure.

Below / Llywelyn ap Gruffudd was the last of the Welsh Prince before Edward I took the principality under his control

Although there are clues. The most obvious is its general appearance, the style of its drawings and handwriting. These make it likely to belong to the end of the 13th century. Another clue comes from the Welsh castles, Conway and Caernarvon, which were built by Edward I following his conquest of Wales. It was in 1282 that he finally defeated the last of the Welsh princes, Llywelyn ap Gruffudd, and, two years later, brought the whole principality under his direct rule. As both castles are pictured prominently in the Mappa - they were important at the time, newly splendid and topical - it cannot have been made before that date, or at any rate completed; the work would have taken several years. So the Mappa was probably made sometime in the last fifteen years of the 13th century. It is not possible to be more exact. At least there is no doubt about its creator. There is a message from him, in Norman French, in the lower left hand corner, asking for all who see or read his 'estoire' to pray to Jesus for pity on Richard of Haldingham and Lafford who has made it and drawn it, that joy in Heaven be granted him.

But who was this Richard of the Map? Haldingham and Lafford are the old names of the parishes of Holdingham and Sleaford in Lincolnshire. Certainly, in the Map, Richard made a point of featuring Lincoln, his home ground, importantly, rather disproportionately so in fact. We can tell from his use of Norman French that he was not simply a humble scribe working under orders, but more the designer and director of the Map, an educated man, a churchman perhaps. Records show that from 1278 to 1283 there was a prebendary, a senior churchman, called Richard de Bello, attached to Lincoln Cathedral. Two decades later, in 1305, there was a Canon Richard de Bello at Hereford Cathedral. It

Below / Was Lincoln the home of the Mappa's designer?

18

is possible that these two Richards were the same, possible too that he was the creator of the Map, which he brought with him when he moved to Hereford. That could also explain the sketchy drawing of Hereford, particularly compared to Lincoln, indicating that perhaps it was added as an afterthought when the Map was transferred.

Another possibility is that these two Richard de Bellos were related and the Mappa was passed on through the family. Yet another theory suggests that the Mappa is a copy of a much earlier map, one dating from the mid 12th century, which is listed in a catalogue of medieval books at Lincoln Cathedral. So it could be that Richard de Bello was neither involved in the making of the Map at all, nor in bringing it to Hereford. In which case why would it have been moved from Lincoln? One reason could have been its importance as a teaching aid. In the early Middle Ages cathedrals were the main centres of learning. Cathedral Chancellors licensed schools and teachers in the diocese; they organised the training of choristers and clerks, as well as the cathedral grammar schools. All of which proved usefully profitable. But with the rise of the new universities the cathedrals began to lose ground. Competition built up, and rivalry. The acquisition of a fine encyclopaedic wall map, perhaps the finest of them all, would have raised Hereford's standing in the education stakes as much as a state-of-the-art science block would today.

Perhaps it did. Perhaps the Mappa was hung in pride of place, was studied and admired for many years, centuries even. No one knows.

And when did it first come to Hereford? There is no record of it being there, nothing at all, until late in the 17th century. Then, in about 1682, a researcher, Thomas Dingley, came across it in the Cathedral Library. Briefly in his book, *History of Marble*, he mentioned 'a map of ye world' which he found 'among other curiosities'. He described it as being 'kept in a frame with two doors, with gilded

FOCUS

In the early Middle Ages cathedrals were the main centres of learning. Cathedral Chancellors licensed schools and teachers in the diocese.

and painted letters and figures'. Which suggests it had been made into an altar screen. And, in fact it seems likely that it was, for in 1348, when the Black Death spread through the country, so many people died that cathedrals had to set up extra altars to cope with the rush of funerals. By that stage, with the cathedrals eclipsed by the universities, the Mappa would have become redundant as a teaching aid. So why not, the canons of Hereford may have asked, frame it and use it as an altar screen?

But eventually, when the plague was over and life, and the death rate, returned to normal, what happened to it then?

Perhaps, with the growth of chantries at that time, it continued to be useful as an altar screen, possibly right up to the Reformation when it would almost certainly have been removed. Or perhaps, as long ago as that, it was put away in the library among other treasures, the 'other curiosities' as Thomas Dingley called them. Perhaps it was displayed, if there was space. Or perhaps it was folded, its two doors closed, propped in a corner gathering dust, increasingly forgotten as time went by. Sadly it is easy to imagine so.

For there it stayed in its triptych frame in the Library until early in the 19th century. Once, in 1770, an art historian, Richard Gough noted it was there; 'a very curious map which formerly served as an altar piece'. And at about the same time an artist, John Carter, drew a sketch of it, which was recently discovered in the British Library. Otherwise how many looked at it? How many even knew that it was there? Certainly nothing was heard of it.

Then in 1820 it was moved into the vestry. At last it was starting to be noticed. Here was something rather special, historically important, something rare and valuable. It was lent to the Royal Geographical Society and later, in 1859, after it had been restored by the British Museum, to an exhibition in Manchester. In 1862 it was put on view at the International Exhibition in London. People, thousands, came to gaze at it, to find themselves caught up in its mystery. The Mappa was beginning to be great again.

When it returned to Hereford it was displayed in the South Choir aisle of the Cathedral until the Second World War, when it was sent away to be kept in safety. All this time it was still in its old triptych frame, but finally, in 1946, when it was again restored, a new wooden case was made for it. (Recent carbon dating tests proved that the back panel of the old frame was roughly contemporary with the Map.) Then, back in Hereford where it belonged, it was hung in the North Choir Aisle of the Cathedral. But the story was not over. It was not, at that stage, happy ever after.

Left / An imaginary reconstruction from the 19th century, of the ancient west front of Hereford Cathedral

All ancient Cathedrals need continual maintenance to keep the fabric of the building in good repair. Hereford, dating back to the 11th century, is built of soft sandstone which the weather and, increasingly, pollution quickly cause to deteriorate. Repair work is expensive; major repairs to a roof, a tower, cost enormous sums. Until recently the government gave no financial help. Extra funds can be raised by organised appeals, charity events such as concerts and bazaars. Another way, more drastic and generally more controversial, is by selling one of the Cathedral treasures. In the late 1990's that is what Hereford decided to do. They decided to sell the Mappa Mundi.

The decision was not easy. Many people were strongly opposed. The Mappa was unique, seen as the Cathedral's greatest treasure. On the other hand, it was argued, the Cathedral itself was greater still and if the necessary repairs were not carried out, particularly to the massive stone tower, the whole building would become unsafe.

So the Mappa was sent for auction. Feelings ran high. Had the decision to sell been right? It was an anxious time. Inside the Cathedral prayers were said, desperate prayers. A miracle was needed. Then one happened.

Above / A curiously insignificant Hereford on the River Wye

In 1991 a donation arrived, a donation so generous it really did seem like a miracle. It was specifically targeted towards a new building close to the Cathedral which would house both the Mappa Mundi and the historic libraries of medieval books and manuscripts. At around the same time grants became available towards the cost of ongoing repairs to the Cathedral.

So the happy ending has come about and everyone, not only the people of Hereford, but others who visit from around the world, must be grateful the Mappa has been saved.

And if Richard of Haldingham and Lafford could see his creation in its fine new home, how honoured he would feel, how pleased and proud.

Perhaps he can.

T H E   M A P

GEOGRAPHY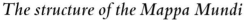

The structure of the Mappa Mundi

AT FIRST SIGHT THE GEOGRAPHY of a medieval mappa mundi makes no sense. The outline of the land, the islands, oceans, seem entirely strange. It could be the surface of the moon. This is certainly true of the Hereford Mappa Mundi. Its world is a great irregular island dissected by rivers and inland seas. Like most encyclopaedic maps it was made according to the Tripartite plan; a world of three continents enclosed within a circular frame. This traditional form set limits on the designer of the map forcing him into distortions of scale and distance. It may well have been that he knew more about the size, shape and extent of the world than he was able to include. In any case the actual geography of the map mattered less than what it contained; the size of a place was ruled by its importance. Yet, despite these distortions, once you have sorted out the compass points – east is at the top, the world is lying on its side – you begin to see that places are generally in relation to one another.

York is east of Durham. Paris is north west of Rome. So that although distances were hard to judge it would have been quite possible to work out an itinerary from the Mappa by tracing a route from town to town.

Above / Svilla, a representation of the Scilly Isles, using the face and name of the monster that guards the waters between Italy and Sicily

Indeed it seems that perhaps some travellers did so for, looking closely at the Mappa, you see that Paris, the great centre of Europe, is criss-crossed with scratches as if pointing fingers had been drawn across it this way and that. Towns and cities are depicted by buildings; castles, towers, temples, domes, depending on the locality. Many towns stand beside rivers, set firmly on one or other bank, and always facing inwards as if they had been drawn from mid stream. In some cases, where space was short, towns were drawn upside down.

The Mappa is veined with rivers and some appear enormously wide; originally they were painted blue.

Travellers could make use of rivers, following their course, even sailing along them where possible.

Below / Mountains, looking a little like scalloped lace, occur throughout the Mappa. Some, like Snowdon, are quite large with pronounced peaks.

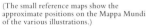

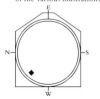

Mountains are clearly marked throughout the Mappa. Sometimes a mountain range is named as a single rise, Snowdon, for example, and Mount Taurus. In places the more prominent ranges are shown to form boundaries, barriers between two lands. The Alps cut off France from Italy, the Pyrenees divide her from Spain. Mountain ranges are drawn as long lines of even humps, sometimes, indicating steepness with small points an top. For single peaks the humps are piled into a pyramid. Each hump is identical, evenly rounded like scalloped lace, which makes them appear as gentle hills.

Wise travellers would have avoided them.

The British Isles

In the far north west, barely inside the rim of the world, Great Britain and Ireland, elongated and kidney-shaped, lie along the western coast of France so that curiously Kent is opposite Acquitaine. Scotland is separated from England by a mighty river Tweed. Cornwall, with part of Devon, is severed from the mainland by the river Exe, and Wales is all but cut off from England by the river Severn and the Dee which meet at Clee Hill. It has been established that the name, Clee Hill, shown correctly

(The small reference maps show the approximate positions on the Mappa Mundi of the various illustrations.)

The Hereford Mappa Mundi

A schematic view showing major landmasses, places, people and beasts

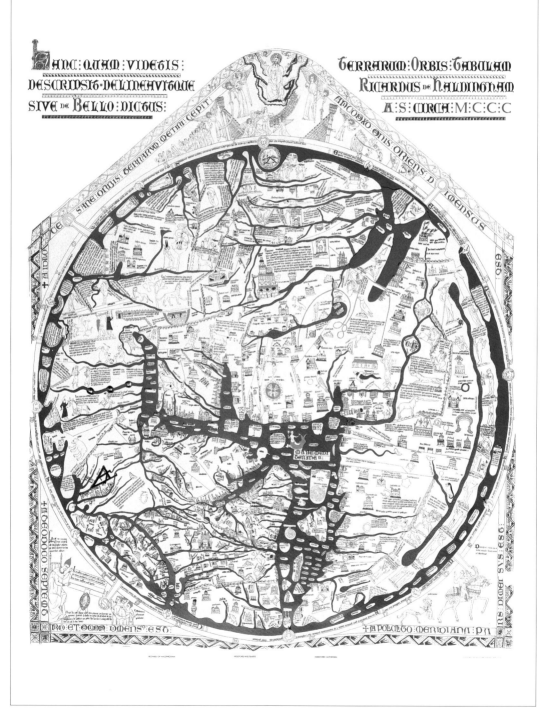

The Hereford Mappa Mundi

A photograph of the map itself in Hereford Cathedral

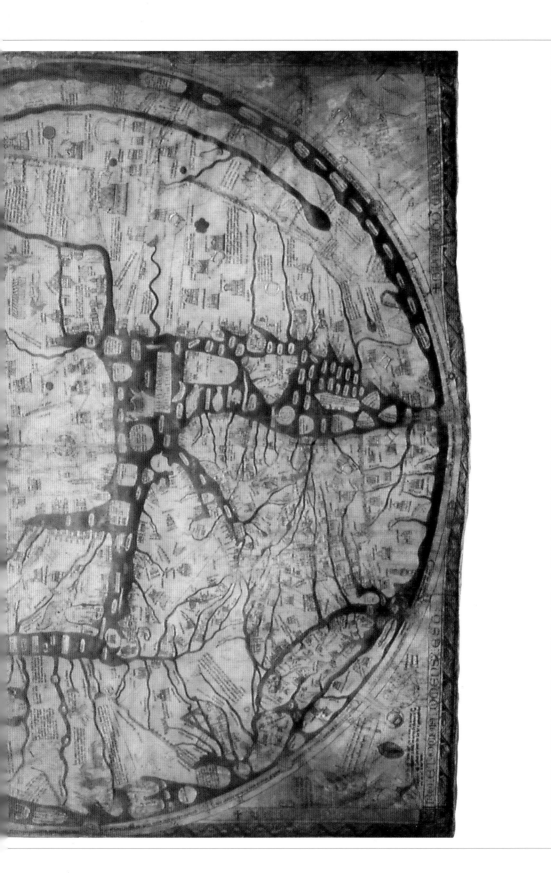

The Hereford Mappa Mundi

A detail showing Christ at the very apex of the map

near Ludlow in Shropshire, was added later, probably after the Mappa had come to Hereford.

According to the Mappa 13th century Britain was evenly peppered with cities and towns. The buildings that mark each one vary markedly in size. Some are small and insignificant, others stand out, large and impressive. The difference does not always reflect the size of the town, but it does seem likely that the places familiar to the designer of the Mappa were drawn in most detail and were probably of actual buildings. Lincoln in particular, which is thought to be his home town, is an elaborate castle on a wooded hill beside the river Witham. In size it nearly equals the Tower of London with its four turrets and massive keep, which is planted firmly on the south bank of the Thames dwarfing a very small Oxford, shown up-stream on the opposite bank. Perhaps the university was still too new to merit anything more impressive. Or perhaps the designer of the Mappa bore a grudge against the town. In which case he must have felt the same about Winchester,

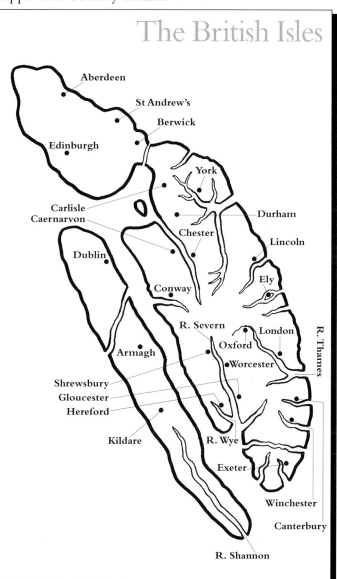

The British Isles

The British Isles showing the locations of towns, cities and rivers. The map is orientated in approximately the same direction as it appears on the Mappa.

Right / The River Severn and surroundings, showing Shrewsbury, Worcester, Gloucester, Hereford - looking quite insignificant - and Clee Hill

Below / London, with a magnificent representation of the Tower, Oxford and the River Thames

Below / The North of England showing Carlisle, York, Durham and Chester. In Wales the two castles are Conway and Caernarvon with Snowdon dominating the rest.

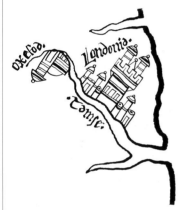

for surely the ancient capital of Wessex was worthy of more than a dumpy little castle. Slightly to the east Canterbury's great keep looks enormous in comparison. Further north the pointed spire of Ely rises from an island in a river named as the Nene. Over in the west Gloucester and Worcester are rugged castles bordering the Severn. Shrewsbury stands guard on the northern bank. But, not far away, sadly and mystifyingly, Hereford looks like a dilapidated barn about to collapse into the river Wye.

Chester, several times the size, is a vast stronghold facing west, perhaps to keep out the marauding Welsh. Durham's castle stands on a hill half hidden in the trees. Nearby is York, a mighty fortress beside the Ouse.

North of the Scottish border Berwick's immense turreted tower keeps watch across the Tweed. Edinburgh stands strong and square on its wooded mound. To the east is Saint Andrew's and, guarding the coast against invaders, a massive fort marks Aberdeen. The Grampian mountains fill the Highlands, range upon range of scalloped humps. In Wales too a solid wedge of mountains named as Snowdon occupies the north. To the south are Edward I's fine new castles, Conway and Caernarvon. Across the narrow Irish Sea, Dublin stands impressively right on the coast surrounded by woods. To the west large castles mark Kildare and Armagh and below them the river Shannon, so wide it seems to split the land

in two, flows away to the open sea. Off the tip of Cornwall are scattered islands and, among them, is the head of a fire-breathing monster labelled Scilla. The Scilly Isles perhaps. Or a touch of confusion. Between the island of Sicily and Italy the whirlpool of Charybdis is guarded by a monster. Its name is Scilla.

Left / Scotland, with Aberdeen and Edinburgh - on a wooded mound - St Andrew's and Berwick astride the River Tweed

Western Europe

Something strange has happened to the coast of western Europe. It has been compressed, the north shunted forward, the contours smoothed. The jutting promontories of Brittany have disappeared and the Bay of Biscay is no more then an inlet. From northern Germany to far west Spain the entire shoreline has been reshaped into a curving bay.

The Mappa shows a Europe closely lined with rivers. A network of them cross the north German plain, linking further south with the Danube and its many tributaries. Vienna is a tower on its southern bank, but Prague, standing alone slightly to the left, has lost its river Vltava. Near the north German coast a row of small towns shelter between the river Weser and the Elbe. Then below them an enormous plain stretches westwards to the Rhine which branches off into yet more rivers.

The Rhine valley is full of towns; towers and domes with one or two castles are lined up along the river banks. Towns guard the coast of northern France and further south, pinpointing Brittany, is Mont Saint Michele, a steep mountain tucked into the shore; no sign of its rocky peninsular. Of all the cities of western Europe the Mappa leaves no doubt which takes pride of place. Paris. The great metropolis of medieval times is shown as a magnificent castle towering over the gothic spire of Sainte Chapelle. Together they stand on the Isle de la Cité in the river Seine. Nearby is Rheims and, with an accurate drawing of a Romanesque church on top of a hill, the town of Laon.

Beyond the Pyrenees is the Spanish city of Santiago de Compostella. There the shrine to Saint James was the most important centre for pilgrimage after the Holy Land. Not far away, at the port of Perara on the Atlantic coast, is the Shrine of the Apostle, an immense lighthouse with flames shooting from the top. It commemorates the spot where the body of Saint James was landed before being taken on to Compostella, the capital of the province of Galicia. To the south of this region the western coast of Spain, is of course what we know as Portugal. In fact the kingdom of Portugal was established as early as 1139, but though the Mappa was made well after that, its geography was based on learning from an earlier time. Spain's greatest river is shown to be the Ebro, which flows from the Pyrenees into the Mediterranean. The Douro and the Minho run west to the Atlantic. Towns are more scattered than in France but to judge by their size they are places of importance. Toledo, near the Pyrenees, stands out, as does Seville further west. Some of the architecture has a Moorish look; domed temples, richly patterned and probably square-based, though from the drawings that is hard

Below / The magnificence of Europe's pre-eminent city, Paris, on the River Seine

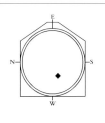

to tell. A number of buildings have conical towers like dunces caps. And to the east across the Alps, in the ankle of the very foreshortened boot of Italy, is Lake Garda with a tributary leading into the river Po. In between them sits Milan, a circular building with high arched windows, like a mini coliseum. A touch of the Roman Empire.

The Mediterranean

The Mediterranean; it is the Mare Medi Teranea, the sea in the middle of the earth. It dominates the Mappa Mundi, a great expanse of darkness, widening and spreading across the world. From close to the western limit of the Map, through the straits of Gibraltar, which separate Europe from Africa, it reaches as far as the Holy Land. There it turns northwards, a huge arm thrusting through the land, pushing out branches to form smaller seas; first the Aegean then, ultimately, beyond Asia Minor, the Black Sea.

It is crammed with islands, this Mare Medi Teranea. They come in all sizes; small ones are everywhere, filling the spaces, rows of them line the coast of Africa. Farthest west are the larger Balearics, all three the same size. A note describes the people of Minorca as famous for their skill with the sling. Next comes Corsica with Sardinia, like a long flat shoe, then an enormous Sicily with Mount Etna erupting in wild flames. Beyond it is Crete, shield–shaped, huge, lying off the toe of Italy. Near the mouth of the Adriatic is Delos, an island sacred to the early Greeks. It is ringed with tiny circles, probably to show that it was once recognised as the centre of the world. Most early medieval maps placed it there and it was not until after about 1120 that the centre was changed to Jerusalem.

Above / Crete with the famous labyrinth of the Minotaur in Knossus

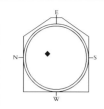

At the eastern end of the Mediterranean is the large bulge of the Holy Land, so large, due to its importance, that Asia Minor, on its left, is reduced in size. It is a region where almost every town is connected with the Bible – along the north shore of the Aegean the names read like a role call from the Acts of the Apostles – where the buildings are domed temples, richly decorated in Byzantine style. So many stand out; Gerera, a wonderfully elaborate temple near the southern shore of the Holy Land, which according to the writings of Saint Jerome[1], was once the leading city of that area, Antioch with its three majestic towers, slightly east of the Aegean, and Constantinople which is drawn upside down on a promontory, near the mouth of the Black Sea. On its left is the enormous delta of the Danube, which flows into it from the west.

Off the north shore of Africa the great lighthouse of Alexandria looks out from the island of Pharos. It was one of the wonders of the ancient world. On its western side is the delta of the Nile. Along the Mediterranean's African coast the small domed towers stand shoulder to shoulder as if everyone chose to live by the sea. Behind them to the south towns are sparse; it is desert land. Long before the Mappa was made, as far back as the 3rd century BC., records show that many of these towns were key points on the routes of the soldiers[2] of the Roman Empire. Carthage, the ancient trading port, dominates the African coast. It was founded but so long ago, in 814 BC., that this counts more as legend than history. But the Mappa shows a fortress that is real enough; indomitable and magnificent it stands guard on its promontory.

Across the sea on the European side Greece appears empty. But the Adriatic waterfront is lined with

Below / The great city of Antioch was visited by St Peter in the first century AD.

towns on either side. Venice is an island right in the middle. Besides its importance as a trading centre it was a busy embarkation port for Pilgrims to Rome and the Holy Land. On the east coast of Greece Athens is a pointed tower set lopsidedly on the shore and, inland, Corinth seems to be lying on its side.

In France Narbonne catches your eye with its single turret on a fat, round tower, and in Spain Tarragona looks like a festive paper crown. Near the straits of Gibraltar are Cordova and Valencia.

But of all the cities on the European coast Rome reigns supreme. It is drawn in great detail, a massive fortress on the river Tiber. It stands opposite Carthage on the African coast. Rome and Carthage, the two mighty cities of the Mare Medi Teranea.

Above / Rome, the eternal city, sits in majesty on the River Tiber.

Africa, Asia and Northern Europe

The continent of Africa fills almost half the Mappa Mundi. From the coast of the Mediterranean it spreads and spreads, fanning out until it reaches the narrow sea that surrounds the world. In the Middle Ages these outer regions were so remote from western Europe and the Middle East that they were virtually unknown. Only very few of the most daring and determined travellers had ventured there – and reported back. So it is not surprising that the Mappa shows these areas as relatively empty and with rivers and mountains set out rather randomly. What is surprising is how close much of it comes to being right.

The Atlas mountains, for example, which are in fact a whole system of ranges running across north west Africa, are marked by a steep mountain on the Atlantic coast where they rightly begin, and then again as a separate range further to the south. They

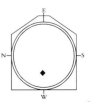

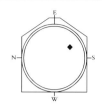

act as a boundary dividing the lands of the Roman Empire in the north from inland Africa, the untamed south. This region contains the enormously wide upper Nile, but very little else.

Among the many islands in the outer seas, and again roughly where they should be, are the Canary Islands. Grand Canary is said to be full of large dogs.

Further east, between the upper Nile and the mountains of Ethiopia there are one or two towns, marked by richly patterned, rather exotic buildings, one with a pair of birds perched on its roof. Beyond these mountains is the boundary between Africa and Asia. Further north is the lower Nile which rises in the east near the Red Sea and flows westwards through the Nubian mountains and the land of Egypt, eventually turning north towards its delta on the Mediterranean. On the south side of the lower Nile just below the Nubian mountains are two small and enchanting churches side by side. They mark the monastery of Saint Anthony[3] who lived in the third century. As it makes its way through Egypt the Nile bulges into two large islands, like a snake swallowing an egg. On one of these islands is an elaborate castle representing Cairo.

Below / A confusingly named Cairo sits on an island in the middle of the Nile.

From here eastwards there is no shortage of towns. This was well known landscape, Old Testament country and almost every name has a biblical connection. Decorative temples stand in a row between the Nile and the Red Sea; a line of forts stand guard along its southern shore.

The Red Sea, which is shaped like a great two pronged tooth, divides Egypt and Nubia from India. At its mouth, where it meets the Indian Ocean, lies the island of Ceylon. Beside it a text explains that Ceylon has two summers, two winters and two springs, and it abounds in elephants.

Broad rivers carve their way across India; the Ganges, rising far to the east in the Osca mountains, the Hydaspes and the Indus flowing south.

Another long chunk of text, a comprehensive fact sheet, describes India's 5,000 cities, its varied population, beasts as well as humans, its abundance of metals and precious stone. These are the lands conquered by Alexander the Great during his Indian campaigns in the 4th century BC. The town of Bucephala is marked; it is where his famous horse, Bucephalus died after the battle of Hydaspes in 325 BC.

To the north of India, beyond the Osca mountains, is China. Here, except for two or three towns sheltering below the mountains, there is only one city, a magnificent building with a conical tower. It is Samarkand.

It was to this part of Asia that the Venetian adventurer, Marco Polo, came in the second half of the 13th century, almost certainly before the Mappa was made. For many years he was employed by the great Mongol emperor, Kublai Kahn, travelling as an emissary all over Asia. He left China in 1292 and afterwards wrote a detailed account of his travels which, until the 19th century, was the only source of information on the geography of the Far East and Asia. But it must have become available too late for the designer of the Mappa. For him the north east region, from Samarkand to the outer sea, was, like southern Africa, unknown land. Generally people imagined it to be too bleak, too snowbound for normal human existence. There is not one town.

Below Samarkand the river Oxus rises and flows northwards into the Caspian Sea, which looks like a key fitted into the edge of the world. Two or three towns stand rather sedately round its southern shore, but below, to the west, scalloped hills show that this is mountain country, so again there are no towns. Among the mountains are the Caspian Gates, a narrow pass through to Armenia and the Black Sea, and at its south east end Mount Taurus indicates

FOCUS

Following his adventures in China Marco Polo fought for the Venetians against the Genoese and was captured. It was while he was in prison that he wrote about his travels in Asia.

another prominent range.

To the north of the Black Sea is another area which was virtually unknown. Great rivers snake their way across the land from the surrounding ocean; otherwise it is empty, remote, cold, probably like the far north east, believed to be uninhabitable.

Yet, confusingly close, due to the distortions of the Mappa, the compressing of land to fit within the world, are Asia Minor and the Mediterranean with numerous towns and a climate which, in summer at least, was decidedly warm.

To the south of the Black Sea, at its eastern end, the river Tigris rises and flows away eastward towards the city of Babylon. Beyond Babylon the mighty Euphrates winds south east through Arabia towards the Red Sea. On its way it passes the beautiful twin-towered city of Petra. Damascus stands alone, apparently miles from anywhere, between the Euphrates and the river Jordan, which widens to form first the Sea of Galilee and then the Dead Sea. Below the Sea of Galilee is the city of Jericho and below that again is the great circular symbol of Jerusalem. The Holy City in the centre of the world.

Below / Jerusalem – the centre of both the Mappa Mundi and of the known world.

Jerusalem·

CREATURES

Peoples and beasts of the Mappa Mundi

I N THE LOWER LEFT HAND CORNER of the Mappa Mundi a remarkable and strangely elegant figure is seated on a narrow high-backed chair. His legs are crossed a little awkwardly and his long loose gown, hitched above one knee, reveals his finely embroidered shoes.

He wears a beehive hat, sports a small neat beard; his expression is stern. Leaning forward he holds out an enormous document with a seal attached. It appears too heavy for his delicate hands.

But this person is no weakling. He is clearly someone of authority. He is, in fact, Caesar Augustus, the adopted son of Julius Caesar and the first of the Roman emperors. His beehive hat is a papal tiara and the document with its splendid seal is his mandate, his authorised order, for a survey of the world.

Receiving it, respectfully, are three commissioners, Nicodoxus, Theoclitus and Polyclitus, who will see that his orders are carried out.

Caesar Augustus was particularly venerated in the later 13th century owing to The Golden Legend, a popular anthology of the lives of the saints, which was compiled around 1250. In it Caesar Augustus is described as having seen a vision of the Virgin Mary with the infant Christ.

But what is such an exalted figure doing down

Left and Above / The commissioners Nicodoxus, Theoclitus and Polyclitus accept the order to survey the world from the Roman emperor Caesar Augustus

(The small reference maps show the approximate positions on the Mappa Mundi of the various illustrations.)

35

there at the bottom of the Mappa? Surely he should be at the top. The answer is that, like almost every world map at that time, the Mappa is a survey of the Christian world. Augustus orders it to be made, God judges the result. And, underneath the picture of Caesar Augustus the designer of the Mappa asks that all who see his work should pray for him. So God must be included in his Mappa and where else but at the top, high above the world in Paradise. And there he is, Christ in Majesty, seated in the clouds, a symmetrical figure with both arms raised, showing the nail marks in his hands and feet. Below him, inside the gates of Heaven, is the Virgin Mary with her three attendant angels. She is pulling open her gown to show her maidenly breasts, pleading by her mother's milk for her Son to have pity on sinners who have shown devotion to her.

On Christ's left side, where an angel with a long curved trumpet sounds a note of doom, one batch of sinners has already been condemned. Roped together they are being dragged gleefully by a winged devil down the rim of the world towards the head of a terrifying monster with gaping jaws. This is the gate of hell.

On Christ's right side another angel blows his trumpet to welcome the righteous to Paradise. A number of them wait in an orderly queue for the angel on duty to lead them in. At the back of the queue others are emerging from their graves.

The border of the Mappa, the spirit world, is cut off from the living world by the double frame that rings it round. The outer frame is divided into

Above / Christ sits among the clouds at the apex of the Mappa

Below Right / Even Auster, blowing from the south, which according to the Table of the Winds brings forth flowers, has a fiery image

four sections; Oriens, the east, is at the top; Occidens, the west, at the bottom; Septentrio, the north, is on the left and Meridio, the south, is on the right. The inner frame contains the Table of the Winds[1], how they blow, who they are, for all twelve have names. There are Notus, Favonius, Subsolanus, Auster, Eurus and Circius; names that are music on their own. And there are half a dozen more. But whether they are temperate, stormy, wild, each one is portrayed alarmingly. (In this the Hereford Mappa differs from most medieval maps which depict the winds as angels blowing trumpets or cherubs puffing out their cheeks.)

Eight of the winds are fork-tongued dragons breathing fire stationed at intervals around the frame. Between each pair, crouching toad-like above the compass points, is a small, plump devil blowing its evil into the world.

And one must have succeeded, for, at the eastern point, just inside the world, is the Terrestrial Paradise, a round island ringed by flames. It is here that the celestial rivers flow and, standing between two of them, are Adam and Eve accepting an apple, the forbidden fruit, from the wily serpent.

Below the island Adam and Eve[2] appear again under the Green and Dry Tree[3]. An angel, sword in hand, is driving them away from Paradise towards the dog-eared giants, the children of fallen angels, and on into the world below.

That was the beginning, the fall of man, the first of all the incidents connected with the Bible that are pictured in the Mappa. And the story is continued through the old and new testaments with each event in its geographic setting. In the southern part of Asia the Red Sea[4] has parted to allow the Israelites to cross safely to the other side. Their route from Egypt to the promised land is marked by a snaking line that loops around the Sea of Galilee to Jericho. On

Above / Adam and Eve with the Serpent in Paradise, representing the fall from grace

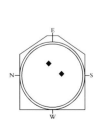

oriea joſeph.

Above / A curiously Welsh looking barn used by Joseph for storing grain

Below / The Tower of Babel rising ever upward from the River Euphrates

the north side of the Red Sea Moses[5] is receiving the tablets of the covenant. Mysteriously he has grown horns. This can probably be explained by confusion over the Latin words cornu, meaning a horn and cornutus, meaning shining. The Book of Exodus describes how when Moses came down from Mount Sinai with the two stone tablets of the Covenant, the skin of his face was shining because he had spoken to God.

Nearby is a building that looks like a traditional Welsh long house. It is the great barn[6] where Joseph stored grain during the seven years of plenty. It is, in fact, probably a drawing of a medieval tithe barn.

To the north of the Red Sea, beside the river Tigris, a face stares through the doorway of a small tabernacle. It is Abraham[7] who was summoned by God from Ur of the Chaldees during his great migration to the land of Canaan. The reason he is pictured in a tabernacle may be due to the story of how he was visited by God as he sat in his tent in the heat of the day. The Latin for tent is tabernacula.

Not far away, and dwarfing everything around it, is what was said to be the tallest building in the world, the Tower of Babel[8]. It rises above the Euphrates river, which reputedly flowed through its foundations, appearing so vast, so crazily detailed it seems that any moment the madness inside it might erupt. Or perhaps that is already beginning for, above the lower battlements, a desperate creature rears its body upwards towards the sky. An extremely long text beside the Tower describes the city of Babylon, its outstanding beauty, its magnificence.

Further north, in the mountainous region of Armenia, is a perfectly symmetrical tub-shaped boat. It is Noah's Ark[9]. The drawing is beautifully detailed and, looking closely, you see how the timber of the hull is woven like basket work, how the heads of the passengers appear through the row of arched portholes; Noah and his family, animals, birds; there is even a snake.

To the south of Noah's ark is the river Jordan where Lot's wife[10] stands forlornly looking back at Sodom and Gomorrah, two piles of bricks, submerged in the Dead Sea. Below her to the west is Jericho[11], where the Israelites, led by Moses, finally ended their wanderings. The Latin text describing this has been copied by a scribe with some very strange spelling.

Not far west of Jericho is the Mount of Olives and beyond it Jerusalem, the hub of the world. It is

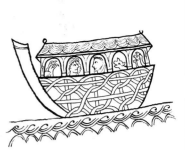

Above / Noah, family and animals at sea in the Ark

a great round city, crowded with buildings and encircled by a wall. Just outside, on Mount Calvary, Christ is crucified[12]. And, among the elaborate temples pictured below, is a very different sort of place, a simple stable. The name above it is Bethleem[13]. But though the Mappa is em-phatically Christian, the Bible is by no means its only source. Much of its learning comes from the time of the Roman Empire and from early classical scholars; Pliny, Solinus, Orosius, Isidore of Seville, names that have a ring of the ancient past however little they may mean to us. Other sources would have been works on the Marvels of the East, also Bestiaries[14], which contained descriptions of different species of animals and which again were mainly based on the works of Greek and Latin scholars. Bestiaries were very popular in medieval times; the illustrations were generally fairly fanciful, with more emphasis on the nature of the animal, its strength, cunning, or ferocity, than on its actual appearance.

But the animals pictured in the Mappa are not treated as symbols; they are drawn in simple,

Left / The stable in Bethlehem – simplicity itself

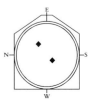

Above / The elephant, a beast of war, with a howdah on its back

Below / An alligator on the banks of a river in India

Right / The Sciapod - one of many bizarre peoples on the Mappa

straightforward style and, considering how little was known about animals from other lands, they look surprisingly real.

Probably the most lifelike is the elephant in the far east region of India. Elephants had for centuries been used in warfare - Hannibal is renowned for crossing the Alps with elephants around 200 BC - and this one is shown as a beast of war with a howdah on his back. One reason the drawing is so convincing may be that from 1255 to 1259 Henry III kept a real elephant in the Tower of London. It must have been a great curiosity.

India is shown as full of creatures of all kinds, real and fantastic. An alligator, or possibly a giant lizard, rests by the banks of the Hydaspes river; nearby a parrot perches on a mound. Then, in the mountains, there is a pair of enormous legendary birds called Alerions, and further east a type of man called the Sciapod, who shelters himself from the burning sun with his one huge foot. Below him are the Gangines with their delicate digestion; their only food is the scent of apples. But there is nothing unreal about the Bactrian camel with its two humps. The text points out that camels do not wear out their hooves.

Further north beyond the river Ganges and the Osca mountains is the land of the Seres - we would call them the Chinese - who, the text explains, make their clothes out of silk. But the creature that stands out in that remote region of the world is the pelican. She is beautifully and realistically drawn, but

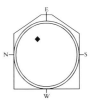

why she is there is not explained. Perhaps it is simply that there is space for her with her three chicks straining upwards from their large round nest eager for food. Curving her neck, she is plucking at her breasts, wounding herself to feed her young on her own flesh and blood. The truth of it is that pelicans only pluck their breasts for down to build nests, but the legend of the bird wounding herself out of love was adopted in the Middle Ages as a symbol of God's compassion. The image of a pelican was often used in the carving and stonework of churches. There is a fine example in the roof of the Bishop's cloisters at Hereford Cathedral.

Beside the pelican is a sinister bird-headed creature leaning on a stave. Just below, on either side of a fig tree with enormous leaves, is the Hyrcanean tiger, famous for its speed and ferocity, and the manticora. This animal, who roamed the western regions of India, has the body of a lion, the face of a man, a scorpion's tail and the voice of a sibyl, a prophetess. Close by, and a very long way from the island of Crete, is the Minotaur, a rather endearing, gentle-looking creature with a large bull head. It stands upright holding the tip of its tail.

Below / The pelican was a potent symbol of God's compassion

Towards the north is the splendid emerald guarding griffin, which is very like a winged Welsh dragon. It is defending itself from attack by several Scythians, brandishing their swords. One Scythian seems to be facing in the wrong direction. Below are two Essendones, eating ravenously. They were a legendary race who feasted on the flesh of their dead parents. Not far away is another creature with peculiar taste, the iron-eating ostrich. And what is it doing in southern Russia?

There are other strange races inhabiting that part of the world; the Grifones, for example, who use the bodies of their enemies as horse-trappings, and the dog-headed men pictured huddled together on a promontory in the outer sea. Perhaps they are too stupid to protect themselves from the bitter cold,

Above / Gansmir the Norwegian stands fully equipped for the frozen north

Below / The Golden fleece '..for the sake of which Jason was sent by King Pelus.'

unlike the Phanesii who live on one of the remote islands and keep warm by wrapping themselves in their enormous ears. More sensibly dressed for the northern climate is the legendary Norwegian, Gansmir, with his skis and ski pole, who wears a full length coat, boots and a pointed snow-hat like a garden gnome. On his right, to the east of the Vistula river, are two lifelike animals, a bear, who might well be prowling through that wooded land, and an ape, who most certainly would not.

One of the most interesting illustrations in the Mappa is the Golden Fleece, which is pictured at Colchis near the eastern end of the Black Sea. The text above reads 'for the sake of which Jason was sent by King Pelus'. The fleece is complete with its head and is shown stretched out, spread-eagled on its front to show its full extent. This would probably have been how the leather skin was stretched in preparation for the making of the Mappa.

In the land of Asia Minor, close to the shore of the Black Sea, is the lynx, a beautiful and somehow mysterious animal with great haunting eyes. It was believed that the lynx could see through walls and that it deposited a black stone of congealed urine which had healing powers.

Further south a far more aggressive beast is the Bonnacan which has the head of a bull, a horse's mane and ram's horns. Anyone rash enough to chase it would be showered with dung, enough to cover three acres and burn what it touched. Perhaps, should that happen, the answer would be to plunge into the Adriatic Sea, not far to the west, and swim down to the Mediterranean. There you could join the mermaid who is large and rather stately and, as is the way with mermaids, holds a mirror ready to admire herself. She is steering towards the island of Rhodes where the Colossus, depicted as a massive column, was one of the wonders of the ancient world.

Below the mermaid is a gigantic swordfish with

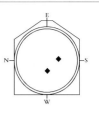

its weapon in its belly, and a monster flat fish that might be a plaice. And in between Sicily and Italy, curled like an ammonite, is the whirlpool, Charybdis, with the monster who guards it, Scilla, or Svilla. The same monster is shown to the south of the British Isles.

Between the Straits of Gibraltar, where the *mare medi* meets the outer seas, two great pillars stand on the island of Gades. They are the Pillars of Hercules. Gades is the sea port of Cadiz shifted sideways a little from south west Spain. According to the legend the Pillars mark the spot where Hercules forced a passage between Europe and Africa to reach Gades.

Not far from the Mediterranean coast of France, between the Alps and the Pyrenees, is an outsize bull. It is an ugly beast and, with its great hooves and curling horns, could be mistaken for a buffalo. It is labelled Bugloss, which in fact is a plant, the herb related to borage with a bright blue flower. The mix–up may have come from the other name of this plant, ox-tongue, being confused with tales of bull fighting brought back by travellers from southern Europe.

On the opposite shore of the Mediterranean, not far from Carthage, Saint Augustine, crowned and robed, sits under his elaborate canopy in his palace at Hippo.

Behind him the great spreading lands of Africa are inhabited by creatures of the strangest kinds.

𝔪𝔞𝔫𝔡𝔯𝔞𝔤𝔬𝔯𝔞 Possibly the mandrake, which here is found growing on the banks of the Nile, counts more as a plant than a living being, but it has a decidedly human face and screams shrilly when pulled from the ground. Its magical powers were said to cure infertility. Close by is a salamander, described as a most poisonous dragon; all who drink

Above / A swordfish with a tidily sheathed sword

Below / Bugloss, whether bull or buffalo, is a little less than handsome

Left / The mandrake is a strange mixture of plant and man

Salamandia.

from the river where it swims will certainly die. Above the salamander is the yale, which we would call a water buffalo, and the phoenix with its brilliant red and gold plumage. Here in Egypt, where it is pictured, this bird was associated with sun worship. Only one phoenix existed at a time; its life span was 500 years.

Above / The salamander is a most dangerous beast, as is the rhinoceros (Right)

Further south are two beasts with single horns; one a rhinoceros, the other a mono-ceros, which is half gazelle and half unicorn with a horn longer than its entire body. It was said that the monoceros, like the traditional unicorn, will lay its head in a virgin's lap. Not far away, enclosed within the mountains of Ethiopia, is the sphinx. Rearing up on her snakelike tail, she lifts her wings turning with a questioning stare, perhaps to ask her riddle. According to mythology the riddle of the sphinx was finally solved by Oedipus.

Below / Another creature from mythology, a strangely serpentine and female Sphinx

Below the sphinx and close to the banks of the upper Nile is an extraordinary bird - or what appears to be a bird, the basilisk. It was said to be hatched from a cock's egg; its heraldic name is the cockatrice. It is sometimes a snake, sometimes a bird, sometimes a mixture of the two. One glance from the basilisk spelled death.

Nearby the Troglodytes crouch in their caves feasting on serpents, their standard fare. Their name comes from the Greek word for a hole and is now sometimes used to describe a person stuck in their habits, resistant to change. The Troglodytes caught wild animals by riding on their backs. Perhaps they are peering out at the lion and leopard with their great waving tails, prancing through the mountains near their cave. And underneath the lion, if you

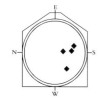

look closely, you may see, tiny and stick-like, the gold-digging ants.

Then beyond the upper Nile in the outer reaches of Africa where, like the furthest Asian lands, the inhabitants seem creatures of a nightmare world. There are people with four eyes, or with their heads beneath their shoulders; these were the Blemyes and the Antropophagi; there are people with no ears and twisted feet, or with one arm protruding from their heads, others who can only take food through reeds. And the Pyslii, who are pictured showing their young to the red-tongued serpents. According to the first century scholar, Pliny, it was the Pyslii who imported poisons to Italy. That may refer to the earliest trade in medicines between Africa and Europe.

Above / An almost heraldic leopard from Africa

These are the monstrous races[15], weird, fantastical, beyond belief. That is how they appear to us. But what of the people of medieval times, how much of the Mappa did they believe? How much was myth and how much real?

Possibly many kept open minds. There were, after all, at the time they lived, witches, alchemists, sorcerers. And even now, seven hundred years later, with all our scientific know-how, who can be sure there is not a Yeti, a Loch Ness monster, a Bodmin beast?

Besides the unknown was closer then – in every sense. And as if to remind those who saw the Mappa how close it was, round the rim of the world, set out like mileposts of passing time, are four single letters, M O R S. It is the Latin word for death.

But at the foot of the Mappa, in the lower right hand corner, is a young horseman on a handsomely caparisoned dappled steed. It is thought he may be the Mappa's designer for he is pictured riding away, as if signing off. Following him is a huntsman with a

FOCUS

Pliny the Elder: his 37 volumes of Natural History, which covered an enormous range of subjects from astrology to zoology, continued to be a major source of scientific knowledge right up to the 17th century.

pair of sprightly greyhounds. The horseman lifts his hand, turning to wave, perhaps to his companion, perhaps to us. Passe Avant, he calls. Go forward. An encouragement? That is how it seems.

We must go forward now. But we have seen the wonders of his Mappa Mundi. We shall not forget.

✤

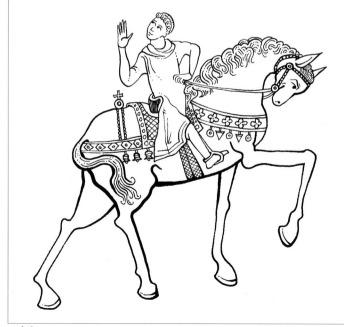

REFERENCES

CHAPTER 1 / HERE BE DRAGONS!

[1]**Sons of Noah**. Genesis, chapter VI, verse 10.

[2]**Jerusalem**. Ezekiel, chapter V, verse 5.

[3]**World Maps**. *History of Cartography*, Bagrow, ed. Skelton, London 1964.

CHAPTER 3 / GEOGRAPHY

[1]**Saint Jerome**. Jerome, (c342–420), Italian by birth, author of the first Latin translation of the Bible from Hebrew as well as biblical commentaries and theological works. Lived as a hermit before being ordained at Antioch. Became secretary to Pope Damasus I from 382 to 385. Later established a monastery in Bethlehem.

[2]**Routes of Roman soldiers**. The Antonine Itineraries: information compiled in the third century on routes of troops of the Roman Empire.

[3]**Saint Anthony**. In 285 Saint Anthony retired to the desert to live as a hermit. Later he founded a community for his disciples who joined him there. *The Sayings of the Desert Fathers*, Benedicta Ward, Mowbray, 1975.

CHAPTER 4 / CREATURES

[1]**Table of the Winds**. Derived from the works of Isidore; names of winds from Orig. xiii II, characters of winds from *De Natura Rerum*.

[2]**Adam and Eve**. Genesis, chapter II, verses 10-14, line 15; Genesis, chapter III, verses 1-7.

[3]**The Green and Dry Tree**. *The Legend of the Green Tree and the Dry*, M.R.Bennett, Archeological Journal, LX, 1926.

[4]**The Red Sea**. Exodus, chapter XIV, verses 21-22.

[5]**Moses**. Exodus, chapter XXXIV, verse 29.

[6]**Joseph's barn**. Genesis, chapter XLI, verses 47-49.

[7]**Abraham**
Genesis, chapter II, verse 31, line 16; Genesis, chapter XVIII, verses 1-2.

[8]**Tower of Babel**. Genesis, chapter XI, verses 1-9.

[9]**Noah's Ark**. Genesis, chapter XIX, verses 23-26.

[10]**Lot's Wife**. Genesis, chapter XIX, verses 23-26.

[11]**Jericho**. Deuteronomy, chapter XXXIV, verses 1-12. The Mappa text tells of Moses leading the people of Israel to Jericho. In the Bible it was under the leadership of his successor, Joshua, that they finally entered the city. *See*: Joshua, chapter VI, verses 20.

[12]**The Crucifixion**. Luke, chapter XXIII, verse 33.

[13]**The Stable at Bethlehem**. Luke, chapter II, verses 5-7.

[14]**Bestiaries**. W.George, *The Bestiary: A Handbook of the Local Fauna*, Archives of Natural History, X, 1981-82.

[15]**The Monstrous Races**. J.D.Friedman, *The Monstrous Races in Medieval Art and Thought*, 1981.